Yes, Mother

A Novel by
Margaret J. Gomez

TATE PUBLISHING, LLC

Acknowledgments

I pay respect and to all who made my book possible: To my deepest thanks to my children, John, Jeanette, Kelly and Michele. To all my brothers, and sisters. To my father for being the only normal parent I had. To all my seven grandchildren. To my grandmother Katherine Sheehan, for being there for me, when I was growing up. To my teacher's at San Jose City College: Ms. Celia Cruz, my counselor Karen Pullen and Ms.Santos. For all the help and support. To the most important person in my life my husband Jesse, for the support and help in making my book possible.

Table of Contents

Some of the names in this book have been changed in order to protect the dignity and privacy of others. This book is not under any circumstances meant to attack or hurt family members. I just want people to know that child abuse happens every day, and could be a direct result of people with some kind of mental illness. If you feel or know of anyone with these conditions, please advise them to seek help. Today, there is help out there for anyone who needs it, you just have to recognize the symptoms and admit it, and not be in denial. Take advantage of this. When I was growing up in the 1950's and 1960's we did not have all the knowledge of these illnesses like we do today. I hope in writing this book, that it will help my family with closure.

Chapter 1

This is a true story of child abuse in the 1950's. Growing up in our family was very distressing because our mother suffered from a sociopathic disorder. That made my life a living nightmare. All of us had to walk on eggshells for years. Mother gave birth to six boys and five girls with a few miscarriages in between. She seemed, from the outside looking in, to be a homemaker for her very large family. Mother did not work outside of the home. Her interactions were phony. Mother would belittle the kids in front of company and make us feel like fools. She had multiple personalities. Everyone thought she was the greatest mom, but the sociopath in her made her do weird and bizarre things. She would have the oldest kid bake a cake from scratch and say that she made it. Mother ordered her children to pay rent for living at home. If we did not, she would threaten to throw us out into the streets. So, I found a babysitting job and raked leaves to get her off my back. When Mother's Day came around, Mother ordered us to buy her gifts. We would say, "What! Why should we?" She did not deserve anything from us. You just cannot do that! Things could not be farther from the truth. We were an Irish Catholic family. Birth control of course, was against the church's beliefs, so Mother continued to conceive one child after another . . .

My father worked seven days a week to provide for his large family. My dad was a tile contractor, and a tile setter. He was away so much, because he was the only one working. He did not love Mother at all. She drove him to drink every night. If he came home early, she would pick on him too. She would call him a good-for-nothing bum. At the time, he was working two jobs, and because of that, he did not know a thing about the abuse that was going on everyday. It became a part of our every-day routine.

There was no stopping of the abuse and fear that we all had to endure all the time. I remember buying underwear with my hard-earned babysitting money. Because I only had one pair, I had to wash every day. I was 14 years old at the time. I went to Woolworth's and bought a few red panties with lace. Mother went wild with rage.

She shouted, "Peggy, come here now, right now. I need to talk with you." I went downstairs. She said, "How dare you! Have you no shame? These panties are for street walkers!" She threw my panties in the fireplace and set them on fire. I was so upset; I had no underwear to wear! The only this I could was to cut my bloomers to fit like underwear. That is pretty much what all the girls had to do.

Another time when I was sixteen years old, I was coming home from school. She asked, "Why are you late coming home today?"

I said, "I was late today because I had detention. I stayed up late doing the dishes last night."

She said, "You are a liar and good-for-nothing fool."

She lifted her foot and kicked me with the heel of her shoe in my inner thigh. The pain was so intense that it brought me to my knees. I bled for a day or so and it turned black and blue. I started to hate her. I stayed away for a few days.

She always left me alone as a small child. One day while I

was attending kindergarten, I got sent home because I was sick. When I got home, Mother was gone again. I cried for hours until someone came home.

Going to school was very unpleasant. I had no lunch. I never had a coat or sweater to wear for those cold chilly days. A sweater would have been welcome on my long walks to school. I did not like my life. I just did not want to go through the same thing day after day. It was hard to wake up and face another day of torture, emotionally and physically. I was neglected and always hungry. It was a vicious circle that repeated day in and day out.

In the 1950's and 60's, child abuse was very common. Child abuse as we know it now was unheard of back then. For us, it went on like clockwork almost every day. It seemed Mother enjoyed torturing us every day. She laughed aloud, and said, "I am glad that now I have children to be my slaves. So I can sit on my fat rear-end."

We were all afraid. We would not tell a soul about our situation. Because if we did, we would get a severe beating and be put to bed without a bite to eat. As far as we were concerned, she was the Devil. One time I remember, she broke my sister Kim's arm because she moved around while she was combing her hair! Broke her arm mind you. Can you imagine that?

All of us would run when we heard her coming down the hall. "Run!" we would say. "Here she comes!" Sometimes, she could not catch up to us because she was a very heavy woman. Nevertheless, when she did, she would kick us, slap us with an open hand, and leave bruises

She changed her mood like night and day. Sometimes she was okay, and sometimes she was fake. She was an evil she-devil. Us kids made a pact, that when we all turned eighteen, we would leave home and never come back for as long as we lived. We never went back home again.

One of my brothers enlisted in the Army during the Vietnam War. He did not care if he lived or died. Mother and Jay really got into it that day. Mother found out that Jay had enlisted in the Army. "Go on" she said. "Eat their food and I hope you come home in a box." Jay cried, and did not return home until 25 years later, after Mother's death.

When I was in high school and still living at home, I had to clean the house, or I could not go anywhere. This house had 13 rooms. That was a lot of work and I was always tired. In order to buy the house, dad got a loan from our family doctor. Mother asked him, "If we are so poor, how can we afford this house?" All the while, she was socking away $1500.00 a month for herself in a separate account so she could go to school. In addition, we wondered why we had no food to eat or clothes to wear.

Mother was such a slob. Her room was so dirty; there was three inches of junk on the floor. There were dirty dishes, dirty clothes, newspapers, food wrappers, and other things I do not want to mention. Mother was about 5' tall and 250 lbs., she looked and acted like a drill sergeant. One time I heard my boyfriend pull up in the driveway. I snuck outside, mother caught me. She was breathing down my neck.

Mother screamed, "Get in here now. You want people to think that you are a streetwalker or something?"

Steve got so mad that he sped away in his car and left tire marks on the driveway.

A few minutes later Mother came out, "Peggy, get the heck in here! Now look what your boyfriend did! Now clean it up."

She told me to find the smallest brush I could find, a toothbrush and a can of Comet cleanser. Well, it took me five hours to clean. I could see Mother looking out the window, smiling. She really loved to torture me.

In the driveway
of our home

That night I went on a date with Steve. I returned at 12:00 A.M. I thought Mother was asleep. She screamed, "Peggy, get the heck in here! Where have you been?"

I told her I had a date.

She said, "I did not give you permission to go anywhere!"

I just rolled my eyes.

She asked, "Where did you go?"

I said, "Just the movies."

Then she asked, "Did he try anything?"

I said, "What do you mean?"

Mother said, "Let me rephrase the question. Did he try to get in your pants?"

I said, "No. Why? We just watched the movie."

Then she asked, "Is he gay?"

Then she ordered, "Turn around. Let me look at you. Are your clothes on the right side? Are all your buttons closed, zippers zipped? Go to bed! I can't stand the sight of you, tramp! I'll

Margaret Gomez

deal with you in the morning."

The next day I woke up to someone looking in my face. It was Mother. She shouted, "Get up, street walker! I have work for you. Get in the bathrooms and start scrubbing the walls and the floors. I want to see my reflection. Do I make myself crystal clear?"

I cried.

She returned. She said, "What the heck is wrong with you? You're lucky you have a roof over your head! Stop complaining and get busy!"

Boy, I hated her. I later snuck out of the house to see my boyfriend. I did not care if I was caught. My boyfriend and I made a plan.

I said, "Get me pregnant. I can't stand living there anymore."

It worked. Months later I felt sick, as if I had the flu. So I made a doctor's appointment, and sure enough I was pregnant. I still felt sick, so I got a prescription for the nausea.

I heard Mother scream, "Peggy, get down here now!" I entered the room. She said, "You look very pale. Well, do you have my rent money?"

I said, "I just threw up. The reason I do not have the rent money is that I spent it on nausea pills. I haven't been feeling well."

"Why?" she asked. "You are not pregnant, are you?"

I said, "Yes, I am."

She went off. She got angry and said, "I knew you were a street walker the day you were born!" I felt like I did not want to live anymore. I just wanted to die. She said, "You have two choices: Give the baby up for adoption or get married."

I said, "No way. I want to keep the baby."

She said, "You tramp. We'll have to plan this wedding very soon, before you start showing." I wanted to get married in the church. Mother said, "You cannot marry in the church! You are pregnant. You will have to get married in the chapel."

The wedding date was set for December 21, 1968. My sister Alice was the maid of honor. My best friend, Linda, was a bridesmaid. Alice was my younger sister she was very shy and had no self-confidence. It was a large wedding, about 250 people. The reception was at home. I could not believe it; I was finally out of Mother's house. There were people standing outside in every room there were extra tables rented for the wedding reception. Mother had one of her neighbors clean up the house for the reception, in exchange she was invited too.

My first child was born in July. He looked like his father; dark complexion, brown eyes, and very dark hair. We decided to name him Joe, after his grandfather. Little Joe had a bad habit of always running around naked. He was two years old when he took off around the block without his clothes; and me, pregnant again with my third child, chased after him. Can you imagine that ?

Months later, I had a baby girl. She had a very light complexion with hazel eyes. She was a very good baby, always a joy. We named her Sue.

I vowed never to be like the mother I had. I was going to be a great mom, and always be there for my kids. One day Mother showed up at my front door, because she heard I was pregnant again. She was the last person I wanted to see. For years, I had blocked her from my mind. I wished she had never stopped by. My mind was flooded with all of my painful memories. The same memories I had skillfully kept locked away inside. Just being in her presence unlocked a door I thought would be closed

Margaret Gomez

forever. She did not stay very long.

She did not say much, but she did ask me, "Why didn't you let me know that you were pregnant?"

"It's none of your business," I said.

She asked, "Why don't you ever come to the house?"

I said, "I don't feel comfortable there."

She gave me a dirty look and left.

I was glad when she left. In her mind, she wanted to play the grandma role. Sociopaths do that. They think there is nothing wrong with their actions. But in my mind, I still had not forgotten what she had done to us kids. It would be hard for me to accept her as a grandmother to my children. She lived about a half-mile from me. My kids knew of their grandmother but did not like her.

In 1972, I was pregnant with my third child, Mary. She had a very dark complexion, light blue eyes, and very long, dark hair. She was very quiet, not much trouble at all. I vowed to break the abuse cycle Mother had created in her household. I never wanted to be like Mother or abuse anyone.

My life was not living up to my dreams. I was married to a drinker that beat me constantly. He was also verbally abusive. One day, he choked me. I could not get his hands off my throat. The kids heard us fighting in the kitchen. So my kids kicked their father so he would stop. To this day, I cannot stand anyone or anything touching my throat. Fifteen years later, I divorced him. It was the best thing I had done in a long time.

My ex-husband said that I would never find anyone. He said that all I would ever be was a tramp. I remember mother would say those same words to me. I felt hurt and cheap I cried. But I got over it and moved on.

I had to learn to do many things for the very first time. I

had to learn how to write a check, gas the car, pay bills, and most importantly, how to stand up for myself. It was not easy raising three kids by myself. I made many mistakes along the way, but it helped me become a stronger person. I worked two jobs, trying to pay rent and the bills. My ex-husband cut off the child support, so I had no income to pay rent for the kids. I could not make the rent, so I was evicted. I asked my ex, "Can you please help me?"

He said, "That's what you get for divorcing me. You get what you deserve." So I had no choice. I had to give up my son and youngest daughter to live with him, while my middle child Sue continued to live with me. I wished I had the money to take him to court to get the child support back, but I did not.

Then one day I met this person at my brother Dick's machine shop in Santa Clara, California. His name was Jim. He worked there, and my brother Jay introduced us. We dated for a while. Then he moved in with me to help pay rent. My daughter asked, "Mom, why is that person living here? I really do not like him." My daughter got in a verbal fight with my boyfriend, so I tried to break it up. The fight was about why he was living with me and that my daughter resented him. He was young enough to be her brother. My daughter was sixteen years old. After that was over, I thought everything was okay. I went outside after that to cool off. I returned an hour later to discover that my daughter moved out. I was so upset that I cried all night. Jim became very abusive. He would beat me, he was very condescending, he would order me around, spend my paychecks and he hated my kids.

I had nightmares and migraines every day. Days did not go by without me thinking about my kids. Jim and I moved to a small suburb called the Dells. It was about fifty miles south of

Madison, Wisconsin. Jim would not let me work. He was very controlling, just like my ex. Boy, I sure know how to pick 'um!

Then two years later, I went back to California, I moved in with my brother Jay until I got back on my feet. The first thing I did when I came back was to see my kids. I rang the doorbell. My youngest daughter answered the door.

"I hate you. Please go away," she said.

She slammed the door. I was very hurt and upset. My kids did not want anything to do with me. It took almost six months for them to come around to see me or talk to me.

We became very close, and then we were like best friends. My kids were teenagers then. Mary was sixteen, Sue was eighteen and they both lived with their father. He was very mean to them, somewhat old-fashioned. The only time he let them go anywhere, was with me, because he knew where they were. I remember when Mary was about 17 years old we were living together. I was just coming home from work. Mary asked if I dated, I said sometimes. She went wild. I was climbing the stairs to my room, and then Mary grabbed my arm, and threw me down a flight of stairs. I slapped her and pulled her hair to get her off me. Mary ripped my blouse and tore my shirt off. I was so shaken up, that I cried.

My body was covered with bruises. I could no believe my own daughter had done this to me. I called my ex-husband, and said,

"I have no place to go." I asked Steve if I could stay at his place. I told him I would explain later. I explained what Mary had done.

He said," You can stay here until you find a place to live."

I moved out in three months. I found a roommate through

a friend. I was working at a car dealership in town.

I did not speak to my daughter Mary for months after she pushed me down the stairs. I worked two jobs for years. It was good I did, because was laid off at the car dealership but continued to work at the Black Angus in Sunnyvale, California. I worked there for two years. Then my sister Alice called one day. I told her I was very unhappy. I needed a change.

So then I moved to Arizona. This time, my kids Joe and Sue took the trip with me. We drove down together, my belongings in tow. The kids stayed with me for a week, and then they flew back home. I put myself through beauty school. Again, I got involved in another bad relationship. His name was Mike, he was an alcoholic. I later had to leave him because he slapped me around and drank too much. You think I would learn the first time but I did not. I left him while he was at work; I took the first fight out that morning. I was so nervous I did not relax until I safely back in my hometown. I was there for two years long years. I found a job at the local super market. This is where met my husband Carlos.

We dated for about four years then decided to get married. That was in September 1987. He is a kind caring person, three years younger than I. I could not believe that there were some nice men out there. I was not used to someone caring and listening to my every word. He is wonderful; maybe I found my soul mate at last. Months later, my ex called, he asked me to come over. He was having a problem with Mary, my youngest daughter. She had locked herself in the bathroom with the baby and would not come out. What was going on was that she was hearing voices. She was later diagnosed with a mental illness called paranoid schizophrenia. It did not show up until she was under a lot of stress. She had many episodes. Her moods were like night and day. Mary was 23 years old then.

One day she really went off. She was admitted to the hospital. She was there for a few weeks and then she was sent home, and began seeing the father of her child again. A few months later, she was pregnant again. She had her second daughter in June. Mary's abusive behavior went on for years. She had very moody behavior, she was violent. She would have episodes of psychotic behavior. She would forget where she was and forget dates, times, and places.

She was living with her father at the time. My ex called me to his house again. Our daughter Mary was walking around the house with a butcher knife in her hand, trying to stab her dad. I called child protection services, and her children were taken to the children's shelter. Then my ex got a court order for my daughter Mary to stay away. Soon after the children were placed in my ex's home. He started adoption procedures for the children, two little girls. I quit my job in order to help with the girls while my ex worked. It was not easy. Mary was always coming around the house, trying to see the girls. Mary was homeless. She would sleep in the streets, in old abandoned cars or old buildings. It made me feel helpless I wanted to help her, but I could not. She was in denial.

One day Mary was picked up for trying to kidnap her children. She was trying to get the kids from school. She was arrested, and put on a 72-hour hold in the mental ward. She then transferred to a mental hospital. She was improving with the help of medication. I visited her every day. One day she got a day pass for the day. Mary went to see her old boyfriend, Chad.

Then one day I was talking to my ex-mother-in-law. She said, "Peggy, I think Mary is pregnant again." I could not believe it! How could this happen again? She was getting bigger every time I saw her.

I was very uncomfortable visiting Mary at the mental hospital. People were like zombies. They were heavily medicated. The place smelled of stench. I felt very uneasy around those people. I did not know if they would attack me or not.

Mary had her third baby girl. She was 5 lbs 4 oz. After the baby was born, the social worker approached me. She asked, "Would you like to adopt the baby?" I did not know what to say. I was just there for the birth of my granddaughter. I talked it over with my husband, Carlos. I really had to think, did I want to raise another child at my age? On the other hand, how could I be selfish and not even consider it? It took a month to decide what I wanted to do.

My husband and I decided to adopt the baby. We had to take four months of kinship and childcare classes. The baby was placed in our home after a thorough background check. We changed her name from Liz to Emily Marie. After that, Mary had her tubes tied. I did not want to go through that again. I worked a 40-hour-a-week job and only got 4 to 5 hours of sleep a night. It was very hard on me, but Emily was worth it. It took one year and many court appearances to make her adoption final. Emily has been with me since she was two weeks old. She is now five years old. She is the younger of her two sisters. She is very smart and out-going, not afraid to try new things. Now she knows how to use a computer. She has her own TV, Xbox games. She has had to grow up fast, because she is the only child in our household. She just started playing soccer. She has a kitten named Pechanga. This is her first year in grade school, she is in kindergarten and she loves it. She says hello to everyone, loves all the teachers and her new classmates.

Margaret Gomez

Chapter 2

My Oldest Brother, Dan

Dan was born in the 1940's while my dad was in the Army. Mother, Dad, and Dan lived at my Aunt's house until they were all kicked out because our mother never cleaned up after herself. . The place was a pigsty, dirty diapers everywhere. Dan was always dirty and neglected by Mother.

A few years later, Ann was born. Mother never took good care of her. Mother was jealous of any female, even her own children. She would starve Ann; that was the beginning of Ann's abuse. Mother's form of punishment for Ann was withholding food from her. Then she would force Ann to watch her older brother eat his meal. She was rarely bathed, and she wore dirty clothing. Our family believes she caused my sister Ann's death at the tender age of two from exposure to a controversial shoe x-ray machine. It was a machine that was used to measure children's feet to size them for shoes. It had too much radiation so they took it off the market. Ann developed leukemia. Mother took her to the shoe store many times. Back in those years, the stores used shoe x-ray machines to check your feet for sizing.

Mother knew the machine was very harmful, but she took her anyway. Months later Ann was covered with bruises and the doctor ran tests. She had cancer. She was so young. There was nothing the doctors could do to help her survive. Ann, my big sister that I never had a chance to meet, died at two years old. She did not have a funeral. Mother said, "They do not have funerals for babies." She was buried in a small grave in California. No

Margaret Gomez

one talked about it again for years. To this day, my father does not talk about it because it makes him sad.

Two years later, Ron was born. He was blond, blue-eyed, and always getting hurt. He was accident-prone. One day, Ron was riding his bike and a car hit him, he was eight years old. I felt so bad he got hurt because he was looking for me. I still can picture the ambulance taking him away. He was okay, just shaken up with a few cuts and bruises.

Two years later Jay was born. He was like Dennis the Menace. He was a joker, always getting into some kind of trouble. The kids were born about every two years. Except Jeremy— there was an eight-year difference him and Tom. That made 11 children in all.

Dan

Yes, Mother

Chapter 3

The Need for Food

The house was so dirty. The floors were either yellow or brown. We could not tell for sure because it had not been mopped in years. The inside of the refrigerator was covered with mold. We had to eat what was inside, or we would starve to death. All we could eat for dinner or lunch was sugar or mayonnaise sandwiches. Sometimes we would eat from the fruit trees in the backyard. One day I passed out at school from lack of food. Mother found out that I had told the school nurse. She slapped me so hard that she made my nose bleed. The teachers thought there were some problems at home. Those days no one talked about it. It was hush-hush. Things were very different then, not like today. Today kids would be taken away and parents arrested.

If we did not do chores, we could not eat. The only real dinner we had was Sunday dinner, which was chicken, lima beans, and potato soup. We all ate slowly because that was the most we would eat all week. If we thought of food, our stomachs ached for more. To this day, I cannot stand lima beans and chunky peanut butter because it was a staple in my life at that time.

At school, we never had a lunch to bring. After the other school kids ate, I would go through the garbage to look for food scraps that kids would not eat. We would steal money out of Mother's purse to buy food on the way home from school. When our aunt would visit, she would take us out for hamburgers. We thought she was the greatest aunt. We could eat. It was the best food we had had in a long time.

Mother and Dad would buy a block of cheese and Italian salami. They would eat it in front of us. I just wanted a taste. They would go out to dinner and not leave us nothing to eat. We all were so thin that our clothes would fall off. We were left unsupervised, always getting into some kind of mischief.

Alice was born in 1953. She was blonde with blue-eyed, just like mother. Mother was always abusing her because she was jealous of her. She had bruises all over her body, like the rest of us—welcome to the club.

If we cursed, she would wash our mouths out with soap or bleach. Mother would say, "I wish you kids were never born! Well, you're here anyway."

Alice was accident-prone. She was always getting hurt. One day she was riding her wonder horse and fell off. Mother did not care; she left the room when it happened. My dad ran into the room.

"What happened?" he asked.

He saw what had happened and took Alice to the hospital. Alice returned with stitches on her eyebrow. She was lucky it was not her eye. Mother did not ask if Alice was okay.

Jay and Ron were playing one day out in the yard. Ron said it would be great to have a dog. They proceeded to take a walk with their wagon. I saw them turning around the corner with their wagon in tow. A few minutes later, they were back. I could not see Ron's face, but it looked like they had something in the wagon. As I got closer to the wagon, I looked inside. It appeared to be a large dog. The dog did not move. I touched the dog with a stick. It was dead. It was full of maggots and ants. Jay and Dan thought it was only asleep. Mother overheard us.

She screamed, "What's in the wagon?" She saw the dog and screamed, "You morons!" She poked it with a stick and confirmed that it was dead. She said, "A dead dog. Nice. Ron, Jay, get in the house now!"

After that, Mother forced my brothers to bathe in diluted bleach. My poor dad; when he got home from work, he had to bury the dog.

We had several fires in the house. I remember one day Jay and I were playing Jack Be Nimble, Jack be Quick. We were jumping over a candlestick. I caught on fire. I was wearing a flannel nightgown. Jay went into the bathroom and threw toilet water on me because we had no running water upstairs. My dad found out, and we got a spanking. I was burned on my arm and legs. Mother did not care, she hid it very well. She just put on kip ointment used for burns and cuts.

Contents of our refridgerator

Jay was always getting into something. One day he made a dummy out of old clothes and shoes, and he stuffed it with newspaper. He got an idea to play in the street in front of the house. He went out to the front of the house, which faces a busy roadway, and put the dummy in front of the street. He then ran into the house.

A few minutes later we hear a car skid and then a voice scream, "Oh, my God. I killed him!" The driver of the car called the police, and they came. They went over to the body. The officer was not pleased.

He said, "This is not a real person. Someone is playing a joke, and it is not funny." My brother Jay was laughing; he did not care. Good thing Mother did not find out or he would have been in a lot of trouble.

Yes, Mother

Pictures of house
where I grew up

Margaret Gomez

Living room

Mother's room

Jeremy's room

Mother was mentally ill. She never should have had children. She would starve us all and never gave it a second thought. In her younger years, she would follow my dad wherever he was stationed while he was in the Army. She thought she really loved him because nobody wanted her. Why did all of us kids have to pay for that?

Mother came from very large Catholic family. Mother's home was three stories high; it consisted of seven bedrooms, 15 rooms total. The home was always kept up and immaculate. Everyone had chores in the home, no matter what age they were. Mother was the oldest child of 13 children. She was raised in a strict Catholic family with very old-fashioned values. Home-cooked meals were made from scratch. Grandma was a full-time homemaker.

I went there as often as I could in the summertime. I would walk straight to Grandma's home from school. She would feed me, and give me the love I lacked in my house. Mother would scream when she found out I went over to Grandma's house. Grandpa worked all the time. He owned his own stocking and uniform shop in downtown San Jose and he was always busy. He was a very quite man and very strict.

Mother was the only odd child in her family. She was strange and had abnormal behavior. We always had to say, "Yes, Mother dear." We all did not like to say it. I hated the thought of looking at her face every day. She never lifted a finger to cook or clean the house. It was a pigsty, smelled of cat urine. There was cat feces in every corner of the room. The kitchen was not fit for humans. There were ants on the counter; dishes piled high in the sink. The food in the cupboard was full of weevils. The food in the refrigerator had mold on everything imaginable. It made you sick to your stomach to look inside. There was not a thing decent to eat, unless you liked mold. At times, the mold in the refrigerator became so bad that the food was covered in a grayish-green haze. Some of the food was swollen with mold. If we had nothing to eat, Mother would say, "Wash off the mold. It's still good!"

Grandma would round up her children, Mother's brothers and sisters, on the weekend and go to Mother's house. Grandma, as well as Mother's brothers and sisters, and all of the kids would work together to clean up the house from head to toe. Sometimes the refrigerator would be cleaned. However, weeks later every thing turned to mold again. Mother would just stand by and watch us cleaning, not seeming to care what was going on. At times, the mold in the refrigerator became so bad that the mold turned into runny watery substance.

Mother did not care about anyone else but herself. She would bark orders to all of her children. She would make us serve her meals in her bedroom on command. My brother Jay hated her so much that he put funny things in her food. Mother did not know or could not taste the stuff that was in her food. She said it was good and asked for more. We all wished were living elsewhere. We were ordered to clean all of the rooms in the house. She was like a drill sergeant. If we refused, she said we would be taken away to a concentration camp like the ones from WWII. We all hated her. Her room smelled so bad, it made your stomach ache. She only bathed once a week. She smelled foul, and reeked of body odor.

Dad was afraid of my mother. She was always abusing him. She treated my dad like one of her children. We cooked meals, washed and folded the clothes. You name it, we did it!

She was the devil herself. She broke arms, dislocated limbs. She would withhold food for no reason. It was sick how she could do all these things to us. We thought it was normal. We did not know her behavior was out of the ordinary compared to other moms.

Mother made a will in 1986 that disowned all of us. When she was sick in 2003, no one knew, not that we would care anyway. Mother was in the hospital in 2003. My older brother Ron called and told me that Mother was in the hospital. I did go that day to see her. I was uneasy at first and thought she was going to be very mean and evil, the way she always was. It was different this time; she did not know who I was. Mother had a hard fall in the hospital, resulting in a severe head trauma, which caused in a brain injury. She had diabetes and acquired sepsis while in the hospital. She got an infection from complications from her diabetes. She very contagious, she also had heart failure, and dementia. I think that was all of it.

I went to the hospital every day. She was still alive and kicking but was not conscious. I hated her for what she did to all of us. The reason I did go, was that I needed closure. I also wanted to see if there was any warmth left inside of this woman who had given birth to me as well as my brothers and sisters. If so, I wanted to be able to take a little bit of that warmth to remember her by.

She was getting weaker every day. Only three of her kids went to the hospital. The others wished she would just die. The charge nurse asked my brother Dan if we should disconnect the life support. One week later she did die. I was free from her emotional scaring at last. She died July 27, 2004. We had her cremated. No one wanted her ashes; they sat in my brother's garage for months. There was a church service, but still only three kids showed up. She was a cold, evil, controlling person. In addition, as always, she won again—leaving the house to The Women's Alliance and Santa Clara University. She had boarders that rented rooms in her house that were attending Santa Clara University. In addition, she left money to the Women's Alliance; she probably was feeling guilty about the abuse she gave us. If any of the children fought the will, we would get a dollar each.

All children were hoping that her estate would be shared among all of us to bring closure and a sense of peace for all of us, but to no avail. We were further tortured from beyond the grave with her final cruel act of disowning her own children. In the end, she chose to give us further grief.

After she died, my brother Ron became the executer of her estate. He had to clean the house to get it ready to put up for sale. There were bugs everywhere, urine-soaked carpets. Human feces everywhere. The pipes were broken and there was no running water. I heard from one of my brothers that mother did not have water or electricity. Why do you think? Maybe because she was having the early signs of dementia. I heard when the paramedics came to take my mother to the hospital; she was dirty and acting irrationally and was not in a normal state of mind. After her death, all of mother's furniture was sold at an estate sale. Some of the children took what they wanted from the house. It took five dumpsters to clear the house of broken down furniture. There was bug-infested dishes, clothing, maggots everywhere and the smell was horrendous. To this day, no can stop feeling the pain, the evil she put on us. We all hate her,

34

we always will.

Mother was a family/marriage counselor (imagine that) She spent the latter part of her life helping others, but not her own family. When we all moved out, she established her own family practice in her own home. Sometimes she was okay, and sometimes she was not. At times she was more disturbed then most of the people she was trying to help. The majority of the people were fresh out of Valley Medical Center for the mentally ill. Mother was manipulative and cunning; she had superficial charm, she was very shallow. Mother was incapable of any type of love. Mother was cold-hearted. We saw a smile on her face only when she was abusing us. She was a very bad person and when she died, no one cared.

Mother was raised a strict Catholic, but she took it one-step further. On Good Friday's we went to mass, but when we got home, it was a different story. Mother made all the children kneel for three hours straight. We were in so much pain our knees and back ached. We thought this was what strict Catholic did on Good Fridays. We despised every holiday. Mother would find more chores for us to do. She would make us clean the attic, shampoo carpets, pull weeds by hand, paint the outside of the house. That is why we despised the holidays, we worked. Normal families enjoyed and celebrated them. We were not allowed to watch television. Mother said it was evil because it was a bad influence and unhealthy. Some of my brothers were caught sneaking out the back door to get away from her. My sister and I were ordered to get them back in the house, we just laughted. When we told mother we could not catch them; we were slapped across the face. So all the children were glad that she died. We all hated the ground she walked on, all of her evil ways. Some of us looked like her and wanted plastic surgery to change our

Margaret Gomez

looks. If only we all were not born or had a different mother, we might be happy today, and lead normal lives.

Mother

Mother (standing) with her sisters

Chapter 5

Last Will and Testament of Mary O'Conner dated February 27, 1986.

I, Mary O'Conner, of Santa Clara County, California, being of sound and disposing mind and memory, and not acting under any duress, menace, fraud or the undue influence of any person whomsoever, and intending hereto dispose of all property which at the time of my death shall be owned by me, do make, publish and declare this to be my Last Will and Testament.

First: I hereby revoke all other and former wills and Codicils to Wills by me made.

Second: I declare that I am not married. I further declare that I was previously married to Tom O'Conner, and that said marriage was dissolved in 1981. I have 10 children the issue of this marriage, namely: Dan O'Conner, Ron O'Conner, Jay O'Conner, Margaret Jean O'Conner, Alice O'Conner, Dick O'Conner, Lynn O'Conner, Kim O'Conner, Paul O'Conner, Tim O'Conner, and Ann O'Conner, deceased. I have no other children, either living or dead.

Third: I hereby declare that the following children are disinherited from my estate and shall receive nothing: Dan O'Conner, Ron O'Conner, Jay O'Conner, Margaret O'Conner, Alice O'Conner, Dick O'Conner, Lynn O'Conner, Kim O'Conner Paul O'Conner, and Tim O'Conner.

Fourth: I hereby give, devise and bequeath all of my personal property, other than my counseling practice, to my sister,

Jan. (This is just a facsimile of the real will. The names were changed as a privacy issue).

Chapter 6

Jeremy Applegate

When Jeremy was born, he almost died. He had the cord wrapped around his neck. He was born at O'Connor Hospital in San Jose, California. He was the youngest of 11 children: 6 boys and 4 girls. He was not a planned birth; just another child lost in the crowd.

Jeremy would bang his head on his crib for attention. My brothers and sister would take turns taking care of him. When Jeremy was two years old, Mother slapped his face so hard it bled. Mother wondered why Jeremy never cried. She thought he enjoyed being slapped so hard. He was left alone too many times.

At four years old, the abuse was really bad. Mother would withhold food for punishment if he did not clean his room. When he was five years old, he fell into the swimming pool. The pool was so dirty, you could not see the bottom of the pool.

It was very scary. No one was home but me. Mother was gone again. Good thing I was home or he would have drowned. I remember looking out the window, I saw Jeremy in the pool. I ran outside, I jumped in—clothes and all—to save him.

Every day there was always something new. At six years old, Jeremy hung from the curtain cord, the cord tightly wrapped around his neck. It was as if he planned it. At seven years old, he had the mumps. Mother went to a wedding and left him alone. When he was ten years old, we had all moved out by then.

One day I remember Jeremy called me. "Peggy, help me."

Mother would not let him go anywhere. He was the only child left home, so she had full power to boss him around without others being around to help. A few times Alice found Jeremy sleeping under a bed. Jeremy was home again without parental supervision. There was never enough food for him to eat. He would pass out in school from lack of food. His clothes were ragged down to his underwear. He ate from the fruit trees in the backyard.

Our parents divorced in 1981. Jeremy was kicked out of the house. He was 14 years old then. He called and asked if he could move in with me when he was sixteen. I thought he was kidding. Two years later, he was at my door. He had just gotten his driver's license and drove nine hours by himself to reach my home. I lived in Oregon at the time. He had a broken-down station wagon, but he made it. He smiled that day, he was happy. He was finally away from that evil mother. We saw movies, had real food, and worked on cars too. He started taking acting classes at the community college. He always wanted to act. I knew this from the beginning. I remember when he was eight years old; he made a claymation movie using a eight millimeter camera. From then on, we knew he would get into acting somehow.

In 1983, he changed his name. His birth name was Paul, but later changed it to Jeremy. He wanted to be an actor. Two years later, he moved to Los Angeles. He got a few small parts in some movies. In 1988, he played in a movie starring Raquel Welch in "Scandals in a Small Town." In 1989, he played a part in the movie "Heathers." In 1990, he was on Hard Copy. In 1996, he had a role in "The Cable Guy" as Serf #4. He also tried out for "What's Eating Gilbert Grape?" but he lost it to Leonardo DiCaprio, because he did not look young enough.

Then he got really depressed. He was in and out of mental

hospitals for years. He spent a lot of time by himself. No one heard from him for years. We all thought he was still playing parts in movies. We also found out he was conserved until his death.

In July 2003, after Mother had died, the family was shocked to hear of his death. He had committed suicide by a gunshot wound. If he would have kept in contact, he might be alive today. I cannot believe he is gone. It is still very painful to me. It's like a bad dream. I am doing a complete investigation on my brother's death. I think his doctors over medicated Jeremy.

I am writing this book in memory of my brother. In addition, it will help with closure. I wish he knew how deeply his family loved him. God bless you, Paul. May you rest in peace with God's love.

two years

2nd grade

4th grade

three years

Jeremy, Kim, Tim

by the pool

Margaret Gomez

41

9 years

Last photos 1998

Another reason why I wrote this book is that I want people to know what we went through. All of the physical and mental abuse. I hope this book will help others with similar problems. I hope it helps them with closure. Writing about it helped me cope a little easier and lifted a big weight off my shoulders.

Chapter 7

Other Siblings

Lynn was born with bad lung, yet today she smokes like a chimney. She is allergic to everything. She lived off fruit cocktail and powdered milk. Mother was mean to her, like the others. She and my sister Kim were always getting into some kind of trouble. One day the housekeeper was watching them when a food fight started. There were potatoes and peas everywhere: on the walls, ceiling, and chandelier. Mother came out of her room and fired the housekeeper on the spot.

Kim and Lynn had boyfriends living upstairs in their bedrooms, and no one knew it. They would sneak out of the windows at night, drink and party all night.

Tim was a drug addict. He was in and out of jail all the time. He stole money, forged checks, and hocked everything he could get his hands on, to support his habits. He was a loser and always will be.

Then there was my brother Dick. He was funny. He was the one we called "smelly" because when he was a small boy, he made a mess his pants. The name stuck, so sometimes it slips out. He had very large ear lobes. My other brothers teased him to tears. He was a good boy. He was very quiet, and kept to himself.

Margaret Gomez

Alice

Jay

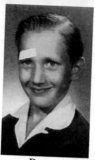

Ron

Dan

Peggy

Dick

Lynn

Kim

Dick, Alice, Ron, Jay, Peggy, Lynn, Dan
1950

Yes, Mother

Tim

Jay, Dan, Peggy, Ron

Ron, Jeremey, Jay

Peggy (author)

Jeremy, Ron

Mary

Ann's grave–died at age 2

Margaret Gomez

As kids growing up, we had many accidents. From bleeding, to fires to almost death. Once there was a fire in Ron and Jay's room.

They were about 11 and 13 years old. They were smoking in their room when they heard Dad coming, so they threw the cigarette under the mattress. Ron and Jay went downstairs, and a few minutes later, Alice screamed. So we all ran upstairs. Oh heck the boys' mattress was on fire! Dad ran up to see. He could not get the mattress down the stairs, so he opened the window and threw it out. Dad then ran down stairs, to the back yard and began hosing down the burning mattress. The boys never smoked in their rooms again. They still smoked but not in the house. They still started fires. They were bored. They would get so bored; they would steal my aunt's car and take it for a joy ride.

Two years later, we had another fire. This time it was on the back porch. The clothes dryer was running. It was a gas dryer, so we had to light it every time. So, could imagine kids playing with matches? Mother never knew or cared what we did. My brother Ron asked Alice to put the matches back on top of the dryer. She thought he meant put them in the dryer, so she did. Alice was only three years old at that time. A half hour later, the whole porch was on fire. We lost all of our clothes. All we had left were the clothes on our backs. So then, we went to go to the Goodwill to find other clothes to wear. It was awful and embarrassing.

We just hate how we lived. We each had only one pair of shoes to wear. The only time we got a new pair was on Easter. That is the only time we had anything new, even if it was only shoes.

Christmas was not the greatest either. The only Christmas

presents we got were from Grandma. The presents were mailed out to us a few weeks before, when Mother was not home. Jay and I would carefully open them to see what we got. Then we would wrap them up again, so no one knew. When Christmas finally came, we acted very surprised.

When I saw all the children in the neighborhood with new toys, I cried. We wished we had a Christmas with new toys, and a mother that cared, and food to eat. Every holiday was the same, wishing we were in a different family. All of the kids were very depressed. We would always be thinking of ways to get out of that house.

Some of us tried suicide; others ran away from home. Alice tried sleeping pills. She took 60 tablets, and was in a coma for three days and almost died. Lynn hitchhiked to LA and almost got raped. Jeremy committed suicide. He was mentally ill too, something we did not find out until later. Jay enlisted in the army. He did not care any more if he lived or died. Tim, the second from the youngest, was always on drugs and still is. I got pregnant to get out.

Alice had to go live at the graveyard once, because she decided to run away from home. She slept in the bushes, stole food from the stores. She showed up at my house, and I called my dad. I could hear mother screaming in the background saying, "I need Alice home to cook and clean the house". Alice was grounded; another one of the punishments Mother gave her. She lost so much weight that she looked very frail.

I once ran away for two weeks and stayed at Dan's house. That was great! I had real food to eat and a clean house to live in. A few weeks later, my dad showed up. It all ended. I had to go back to the other place called "home." It was not pleasant. Mother screamed and grounded me for a month. The only places

I could go to was school and church.

One Sunday I was walking to church, just as if I did every other Sunday. I was ten-years-old. A man pulled over to the curb and asked me for directions. I was telling him where this street was when he grabbed me and pulled me in. I said, "Let me out."

He would not. He drove around for about a half hour. He then took me to this building and told me to get in. So, I did. He said that I could get modeling jobs. Then he started to undress me. I was so young and naïve that I believed him. At that time, I would believe anything to get out of the house. I said to him,

"Please let me go, or I will tell my dad." I told him my dad was a cop. Then he let me go. I ran as fast as I could and never told a soul.

To this day, only a few know what really happened. Years later, when I was fourteen-years-old I remember I had many chores to do. Mother me told to put away the clothes on the back porch. The laundry basket was 3' by 5.' No one put clothes away; they stayed in the basket after they were washed. They were twelve in the family at that time that is why there were so many clothes. It took me hours to finish.

Then after that, I had to clean the kitchen. The dishes were so dirty with food that I could not see the color of the dishes anymore. The cupboards were a mess, bugs in the flour, sugar stuck to the counters and everywhere; it was not fit for humans. It me two hours to clean up all that mess. It seemed she always made me do took the housework, because she was lazy and never cleaned up. I got tired of this, and then I went outside.

I heard my boyfriend's car, got in and took off. I was always sneaking out of the house, and if I got caught, I didn't care. I stayed out later and later. I would have dinner over at my boyfriend Steve's house. We would go to the movies. Around 9:00 P.M. I went home. I still had to do my homework. Mother heard me come in.

She would say, "Where have you been, you little street walker?"

I said, "At Steve's."

She said, "You're grounded."

I said, "You grounded me for a month. Remember?"

She said, "Do not get smart. Shut up and go to bed."

I dreamed I was in a different place. I was always daydreaming. That was the only way I could deal with my life at the time.

The family in 1950

Chapter 8

Coping

The only way I could cope with living with a Mother, that was sociopath, was to trying to block her out. All of the kids would try not to be around her, but that was hard too. She would sniff us out, wherever we were like a dog. Ann died in 1949. She never had a chance. My oldest brother Dan joined the Air Force to get away from her. Ron worked a lot so he would not be home as much. Ron had a hard time dealing with Mother so he turned to alcohol. He was a hard-core drinker. He drank so much, it destroyed his family. When Ron hit rock bottom; he had only twenty cents in his pocket. So, he enrolled at San Jose State, got his degree and became a counselor. He is now doing fine. He is remarried and is very happy.

Jay would always be the family clown. He would make up stories to block mother out. He has had a hard time dealing with his life. Mother really messed him up, very badly. He feels worthless, and feels he will never amount to much. Jay is a machinist now. He is single living in Idaho.

I, too, have had a hard time trusting and believing anyone. Smiling does not come easy for me. I went through many abusive relationships. I have learned through the years to block things out that hurt me. As for the underwear I lost in the fire, I now own at least 40 pairs. I remember getting pregnant to get out of the house. That is how I dealt with it.

Alice could not cope; she was the weakest one of all. She slit her wrists, drank bleach, and do you remember the sleeping pills? The coma? We didn't think she would make it, but she did! She just wanted the pain to go away. She felt cheated from all the good things in her life. She was a loner and hated life. Today she has four children. She still has problems with relationships. All her husbands have been abusive.

Lynn had it tough time too. She has had asthma all her life. Mother hated her because she looked like my dad. She also has a hard time in relationships. She has no self-esteem, feels worthless, and cries at a drop of a hat. She now lives in Oregon with her husband, and is a teacher for kids with special needs.

Dick is a quiet person. He also has had hard times with relationships; he was teased all his life about his earlobes. So, when he grew up, he had otoplasty surgery on his ears. He too felt worthless, and had a low self-esteem. Dick now is remarried and lives in Montana. He is very happy.

Kim has had a hard time also. She cannot trust anyone. She hopes mother's soul is burning in Hades. Kim is glad that Mother is dead, because she was the meanest person on earth. Kim has rheumatoid arthritis and has to exercise everyday to ease her pain. She is single living in Oregon and is a supervisor.

Tim was born with rotten teeth because mother was taking nausea pills while she was pregnant with him. When he was ten-years-old, the dentist pulled out all his teeth. It was very painful for him, he was just a child. He later turned to drugs to ease the pain, as well as the physical and mental abuse. He sold all my dad's paintings, the pool sweep from the swimming pool, anything he could get a hold of to support his habit. He has been in and out of jail. Eventually, he was kicked out of the house. He kept breaking in to sleep or just to find things to steal to buy drugs. The house has since been up for sale and he would still keep breaking in. Just recently, he was arrested for money laundering. That was very sad, because he was married and has one child, who lives in California.

Jeremy is deceased. He commented suicide in 2000. He was troubled all his life, no one knew how much until he shot himself.

My dad was born in Eureka, California in 1917. He had two sisters and one brother. His mother was very sweet, kind soul. His dad drank a lot. My dad is Polish, French and 1/4 Irish. He is a soft-spoken man, very kind and gentle. Dad got tired of my mother chasing him around. He thought he might die in the war, so he married Mother. I remember making his lunch for work: always a sandwich with mustard, tuna and his thermos of coffee. My dad worked very hard to pay the bills and the house payment. Dad never knew about what mother was doing to us until we were grown up and on our own. Mother would scream profanities at my dad, she would kick and hit him like a dog. My dad gave my mother $1500.00 a month for the household but we all wore rags. There was never decent food to eat. That was because mother was putting all the money away for her own personal use. Mother drove my dad nuts; she was always calling my dad a good-for-nothing bum. How could dad take the abuse from her? Why stay with a woman like that? To this day I will never know.

My parents divorced in 1981 but they still lived together. Why you ask? The reason is that my dad was waiting for the house to sell so he could get his half of the house. Mother made his life unbearable, she would actually sleep with a shotgun. Mother threw plates of food at my dad saying "Dinner is served. " He just wanted out of the house before something awful would happen. So the day came my dad got his share of the house. My dad loaded up all he needed and drove up to Eureka, California. I wish Dad had divorced her years ago. All of the children were very close to my dad. He was a normal parent, not like the sociopath mother we had. Dad lived in a small, quiet neighborhood. We all took turns visiting him whenever we could. Dad started dating his old high school sweetheart. They were a great pair. Sue cared for my dad very much. They took trips together, cooked meals together, but yet, they had their own separate homes. One day Sue became very sick; she had a bad heart. She was in and out of the hospital for years. She later died.

My dad took it very hard. To this day, he cries when he talks about her. Today my dad is not well. He has gout, and cancer. My brother Jay moved our dad out of his place in Eureka and in with my brother Dick in Montana. Today Dad is eighty-eight years old living at my brother Dick's place and has around the clock nursing care. I hope Dad sticks around for a while. I could not bear it if I lost my father, the only parent that ever cared for us.

Dad (middle) and siblings

Dad

Kim, Dad, Jeremy

Jeremy, Dad

Dad–88 years

Margaret Gomez

Contact Margaret Gomez
pegsue50@sbcglobal.net

or order more copies of this book

TATE PUBLISHING, LLC

127 East Trade Center Terrace
Mustang, OK 73064

888.361.9473

www.tatepublishing.com